LOBO OF THE TASADAY

WRITTEN AND PHOTOGRAPHED BY

John Nance

PANTHEON BOOKS

NEW YORK

For Gillian and Christopher

Deepest appreciation goes to the Tasaday themselves
for making this book possible. Special thanks go also
to the Panamin Foundation, which enabled me to
visit them; to my family for its support; to the many
friends, journalists, and social scientists, particularly
Douglas Yen, whose insights enhanced my under-
standing; and to Dinah Stevenson, whose editing
helped bring it all together.

Library of Congress Cataloging in Publication Data

Nance, John, 1935-   Lobo of the Tasaday.
Summary: An account of the life of a young boy
belonging to a Stone Age tribe recently discovered in a remote jungle in the Philippines.
1. Lobo—Juvenile literature. 2. Tasaday
(Philippine people)—Biography—Juvenile literature. 3. Tasaday (Philippine people)—Juvenile
literature. [1. Tasaday (Philippine people)
2. Philippines—Native races. 3. Man, Primitive]
I. Title.   DS666.T32N38   959.9'7   81-14113
ISBN 0-394-85007-7   AACR2
ISBN 0-394-95007-1 (lib. bdg.)

${O}$N A RUGGED island in the Philippines live a people who call themselves the Tasaday. *Ta* means "people" in their language, and *saday* is the word for their homeplace, a mountain deep in a remote tropical rain forest. The Tasaday have lived there as far back as anyone can remember. Until recently, they thought they and their friends were the only people on earth.

3

4

Lobo is one of the Tasaday. When these pictures were taken, in the early 1970s, he was about ten years old. The Tasaday do not keep track of months or years, so no one knows Lobo's age for certain.

At that time, there were twenty-six Tasaday. They lived in three caves high on the side of the mountain. Most of the Tasaday's six families stayed in the largest and driest cave. Lobo shared one corner of it with his parents and his brothers.

The caves were used for sleeping and for shelter from the rain. When the weather was good, the Tasaday went into the forest to look for food.

They gathered fruit, nuts, and berries. A favorite food was *biking*, the root of a leafy plant. The best roots were as long as a boy's leg and nearly as big around. Using pointed sticks and their bare hands, the men dug up pieces of *biking* and wrapped them in leaves to carry home.

There was also food in the nearby stream: fish, crabs, tadpoles, and frogs. Frogs were the largest creatures the Tasaday ate.

The children rolled leaves into cones to carry what the adults collected. Sometimes the gatherers nibbled as they worked, but most of the food was taken back to the caves, to be divided among all the Tasaday.

There was usually enough for everyone, except when bad weather kept the people inside the caves for several days. Then the youngest were fed first, even if older people had to go without food. The smallest children needed nourishment most. And if the babies were hungry, their crying filled the caves and troubled everyone.

The Tasaday believed that the forest had been made especially for them to live in and take care of by the Owner of All Things. When the sun—which they called the Eye of Day—was bright, that meant the Owner of All Things was happy. When it rained, that meant he was sad. When he was angry he sent storms: the Big Word and the Fiery Light—thunder and lightning. Some said harsh wind was the Owner's breath. Storms were frightening and dangerous. The Tasaday were careful not to do things that might offend the Owner.

Certain birds were thought to be messengers to and from the Owner. One of Lobo's favorite birds was Lemokan.

The Tasaday could call Lemokan by whistling through their hands to imitate its song. They believed that if Lemokan landed near them, it was a warning of danger, and they should stay wherever they were. If they saw the bird fly by and heard it sing, it was safe to go out. And if they heard the bird sing but did not see it, they could take their chances—go or stay.

The Tasaday were fond of butterflies, too. Sometimes a man would tie a vine thread to a butterfly as a leash for a child to hold. Lobo's grandfather, Kuletaw, said butterflies were gifts from the Owner to make people happy.

The Owner had also given the Tasaday the use of the plants and trees in the forest. When gathering food or playing in the vines, they were careful not to destroy the plants, so they could blossom again. Harming these living things would have made the Owner angry.

The Tasaday asked permission of the spirits that watched over various places before gathering food there. Children were taught special words to please the spirits. They were also taught to be wary, because spirits were unpredictable, and the forest was full of dangers. All the people had countless scars on their knees and feet and hands from rocks, sticks, thorns, thistles. Adults continually warned children to watch out for sharp things.

If a cut became infected, certain leaves and vines were crushed and put on the injury. If it didn't heal and the person got sick, the wisest Tasaday appealed to the spirits and the Owner. But sometimes the sick person died. The Tasaday were deeply saddened to lose that person's smile and helping hands. Human life was especially precious because there were so few people.

The Tasaday knew of only two other groups. Although these people lived in the same forest, the Tasaday did not see them often. Still, they were considered friends. The Tasaday language had no words for "enemy" or "war."

Tasaday parents took their children almost everywhere. That way they could work and still keep an eye on the young ones. Children learned early how to perform various tasks because they watched their parents and copied them.

Making tools was an important task. The Tasaday had no metal, so many of their tools were made of stone. Once the right stone was found, it was chipped or rubbed against other stones to shape it or sharpen the edge. A branch tied on with a vine made a handle.

Some tasks were usually per-
formed by children. They collected the leaves that everyone
wore—soft, smooth ones that
didn't itch or scratch. Whenever a
leaf dried out, it was replaced by a
fresh one. The women wore the
longer leaves for skirts. A man or
older boy tied a vine around his
waist and tucked the ends of a leaf
into it, front and back.

One thing young children were not permitted to do was make fire. Fire-making was usually done by two or three men together. They took turns spinning the end of a smoothed stick against a flat piece of wood. When a wisp of smoke rose from the spinning tip, one of the men put dry moss on the spot.

He blew on it until a flame spurted up. Then the others who were gathered around would laugh and say, "It's done, it's good—it's beautiful!"

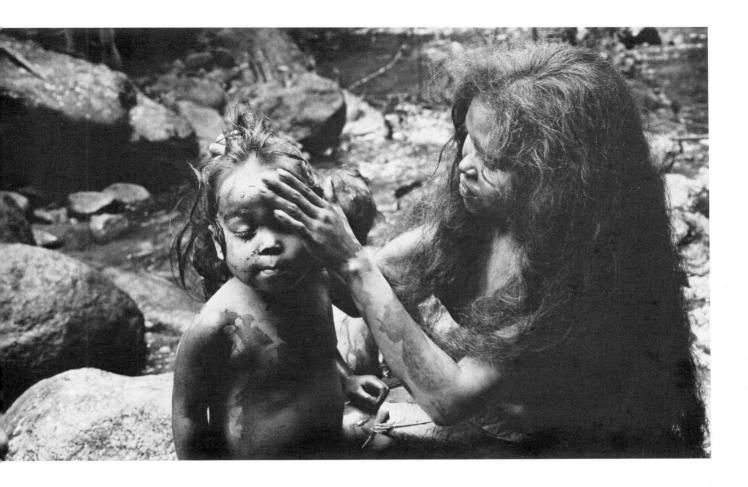

The Tasaday usually spent only a few hours each day working. The stream, important for food and drink, was also a place to play.

Mothers bathed their children after they had slept near the fire and were gray all over from the ashes.

People scrubbed their hair with a bar of sticky clay and used leaves and sand to clean their teeth.

Lobo enjoyed leaping from rock to rock in the stream. It was easier than traveling on land, because trees and bushes didn't get in the way.

The forest, too, was a place to play as well as work. Lobo liked to climb trees and swing from the branches. If he found the right spot, he could close his eyes and rest.

Lobo's favorite pastime was swinging on a long vine. He would tie a stick at the end to stand or sit on. Then he pulled the vine up a slope, climbed on, and swung through the air—almost like flying.

Sometimes children had to look after their younger brothers and sisters. Lobo liked playing with his little brother, Ilib; and while he didn't always like to stop what he was doing to comfort Ilib, he did it anyway. The Tasaday believed that people should help one another. Lobo's father said that this was one of the most important rules of life. It had always been so, he said, since the Owner put the first people in the world.

To the Tasaday, the forest *was* the world. They had never been outside of it; they didn't know there was an outside.

Until the stranger came.

Three Tasaday men were digging *biking* on a wooded hillside when a strange man suddenly stepped from behind a tree. Frightened, the Tasaday dashed away toward their caves. The stranger ran after them, shouting.

They heard some familiar words: "Friends…stop…friend," so they stopped running. They waited nervously as the stranger approached with a smile. He had a dark and bulbous face, carried a bow, and wore pants, a shirt, and a hat. On his hip was a scabbard with a long knife in it. The Tasaday had never seen such things.

The stranger's name was Dafal. He had come to the forest to trap animals and collect herbs, which he would take away to trade. The Tasaday understood very few of his words and knew nothing of trapping, or trading, or any place beyond the forest. But as a friendly gesture, they offered him a piece of a special sweet vine that they liked to chew. This vine was rare, known only to the Tasaday. Dafal found it delicious and believed it would be a profitable item to trade.

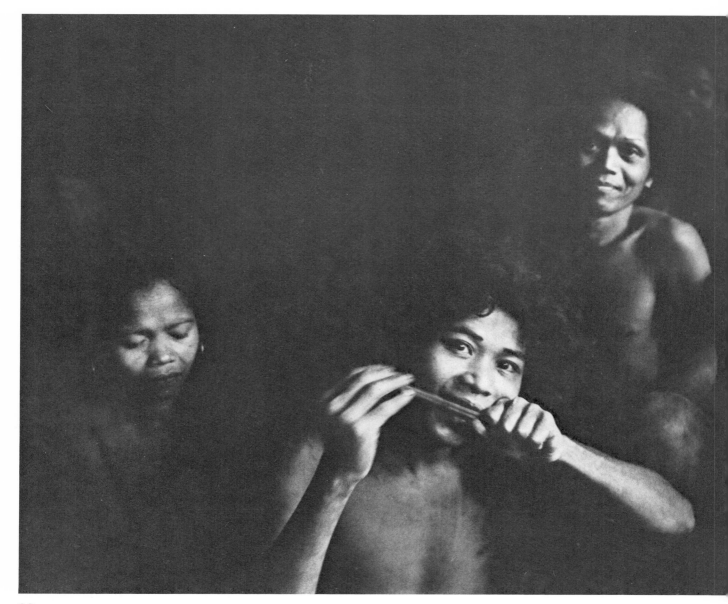

Soon Dafal left, but he returned several times to get more of the sweet vine. In exchange, he gave the Tasaday many things they had never seen before—metal earrings, woven baskets, pieces of cloth. He also gave them a mouth harp carved from bamboo and taught Balayam, Lobo's uncle, to play it. It was the Tasaday's first musical instrument.

Dafal's most exciting gifts were a knife and other small tools made of metal. He taught the Tasaday to sharpen the knife's blade by rubbing it on a flat rock, and amazed them by cutting down a small tree with a few strokes.

31

He showed them how to cut down a large palm tree, split it open, and pound loose the core to produce a food he called *natek*. The Tasaday liked this starchy food so much that from then on they made *natek* whenever they found the right kind of palm tree.

Dafal also showed the Tasaday how he used his bow. Since the Tasaday did not fight or hunt, they had no practical use for such a thing. But Lobo's cousin, Adug, made one as a toy for the younger children.

Dafal set traps to catch pigs and deer and monkeys. The Tasaday worried about killing the animals, some of which they called *kakay,* "friend." Dafal insisted that those creatures had been put in the forest as food for people.

One man agreed to taste Dafal's roasted deer meat. He liked it, and when nothing bad happened to him, others tried it too. The Tasaday concluded that the Owner of All Things and the spirits of the forest approved. Before long, all of the Tasaday enjoyed meat whenever Dafal came. Dafal then taught them to make their own traps, like his, with bamboo spears, thorny branches, and vine triggers.

Although Dafal's tools and traps and ideas proved useful, some Tasaday women did not completely trust him. "We don't know his people or where he comes from," they said.

One day Dafal invited several men to go with him to a place far in the north. He said a powerful man was coming there who would be of great help to the Tasaday. The women argued against going, saying the Tasaday's ancestors had instructed them never to leave their homeplace. To go might anger the Owner, who would send storms and sickness and evil spirits.

Balayam replied that the ancestors had said something else even more important. He recalled a legend that said a good and powerful man would someday bring the Tasaday good fortune.

Others remembered that legend, too. The Tasaday discussed the trip all night. Finally it was agreed that everyone would go. They would see with all of the Tasaday's eyes and hear with all of their ears whether this was truly the good man of their ancestors' legend.

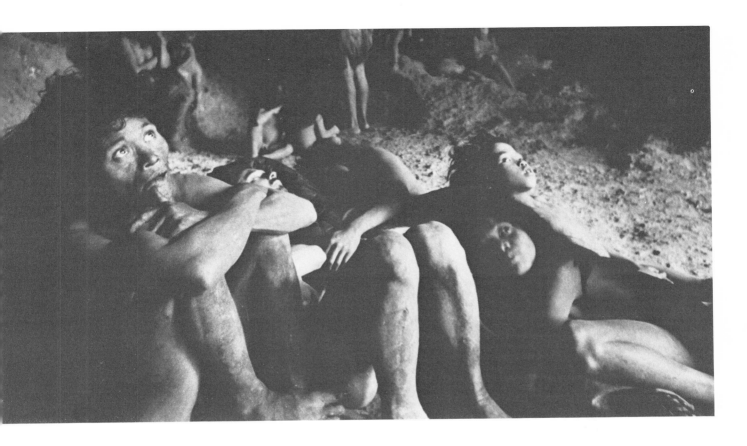

The next morning all twenty-six Tasaday left their caves and followed Dafal. They traveled on trails they knew, found plenty to eat, and slept the first night around fires beside their familiar stream. But the following day they crossed strange mountains and the jungle began to look different. No trails marked the way, and they had to stay in line behind Dafal to keep from getting lost in the dense undergrowth. The night was frightening. Screech owls and shrieking bats kept the travelers awake, fearing that they might have annoyed the spirits of the place.

At dawn the Tasaday moved on eagerly, despite fatigue, sore feet, and insect bites. Lobo's younger brothers cried with hunger, so Lobo and his father searched for food while Etut, their mother, carried both boys. After they found food, rain began to fall, so the men cut palm fronds to cover their families.

When the rain stopped, Dafal urged everyone to resume hiking, because they were near the meeting place. Lobo hurried forward to be close behind Dafal. He climbed a slope thick with trees, bushes, and vines, and found himself at the top of the hill. He looked beyond the summit, and was stunned.

Sweeping down and away from the hilltop was an empty plain that stretched as far as Lobo could see. They had reached the end of the rain forest. To Lobo it looked like the end of the world.

More Tasaday reached the hilltop and looked around. They stared and gasped, then ran back into the forest to hide, confused and frightened by their first sight of the flatland—which they called the Place Where the Eye Sees Too Far.

Dafal coaxed them to come with him, insisting that there was nothing to fear. Finally Balayam agreed to go. Next Lobo's father stepped forward, followed by Kuletaw. Then Lobo, Adug, and a few other men joined them. The rest of the men stayed with the women, who clutched their children and refused to take them any farther.

The small group of Tasaday followed Dafal over the hilltop and onto a grassy knoll overlooking the plain. Soon Dafal began to point into the sky, shouting, "There he is, there he is!" The Tasaday looked and saw only a tiny speck, like an insect flying over the flatland. But as they watched, it grew larger. Then they could hear a humming sound.

Suddenly, the speck was directly overhead. But it was no longer a speck, it was a gigantic creature hovering above them. Its shrill scream hurt their ears and its breath felt like hot wind.

As the monster came down… down…Lobo saw his father running beneath it. Lobo collapsed to the ground in terror and buried his head in his arms.

But suddenly the monster's
breathing and screaming stopped.
Lobo's father helped him to stand
up. Dafal shouted that the good
man would soon appear. A hole
opened in the side of the monster,
now sitting silently in the grass,
and a man climbed out.

He looked odd and fearsome to the Tasaday. On his head sat… what? A large mushroom? He had shiny black eyes that bulged like a frog's. The man put his arm around Kuletaw in greeting, then stepped back and pulled off his black eyes!

Lobo felt so cold and dizzy that he had to sit down. The man came and put a hand on his trembling shoulder, then placed something soft and warm around him.

Lobo's mind was filled with questions. Was this the good man? What would happen to the Tasaday? And the questions were just beginning.

As the hours passed, the Tasaday men gained courage. They even approached the sky monster. Seeing it close up, they thought it must be a huge tame bird.

Over the next few days, the man and the bird brought more strangers and more new things. All of the Tasaday, including the women and small children, came to the clearing. Many received presents of knives and necklaces and food. The Tasaday were astounded by some of the things the strangers brought—silver sticks that produced light, tiny twigs that made fire, one-eyed black boxes that said "ta-suk."

Dafal said the black boxes collected memories for the good man and his friends. Lobo peeked through the eye of one box. He could not understand how it worked, but was pleased to feel the smooth object in his hands.

Later, Lobo even ventured inside the huge bird. He touched the different parts and wondered what they were for.

Dafal asked Lobo if he would like to go up in the sky. Lobo said he would, but not all by himself. Dafal assured him that others would be there, too—Lobo's father, Balayam, Adug, and the good man and some of his friends.

When the bird began to roar, Lobo was frightened again. It shuddered and suddenly rose straight up into the air. It wobbled and swooped over the flatland, then climbed again, higher and higher....

Below him Lobo could see the dark green forest, the flatland, the tiny figures of people. They looked so small, and the world looked so large! The Tasaday's forest was merely part of a much bigger place, which stretched farther than he could see.

It seemed to Lobo that the good man of the ancestors' legend had really come. Lobo's life and the way he looked at the world would never be the same.

AFTERWORD

THE TASADAY discovered and were discovered by the modern world in June, 1971, at the edge of an unmapped mountain rain forest on Mindanao Island in the southern Philippines. No one knows how or why or when the first Tasaday entered that wilderness, but anthropologists estimate that they had lived there for five hundred to a thousand years or more.

The small group of Tasaday had had a Stone Age way of life—without metals, agriculture, wheels, paper, domesticated animals, and many other things we take for granted.

The hunter-trapper Dafal had met them while setting traps in the forest sometime in the 1960s. Dafal guided the Tasaday to the forest's edge in 1971 at the request of Manuel Elizalde, Jr., a Philippine government official and adventurer. Elizalde was on Mindanao to help tribal folk deal with new settlers and modern technology. He believed that loggers, miners, and other exploiters threatened the peace of the Tasaday's forest. One result of the meeting described in this book was that 46,000 acres of the forest were set aside for the exclusive use of the Tasaday.

In December, 1980, a government official said that the forest was still off limits to outsiders, to protect the Tasaday from loggers and others who might bring harm. He reported that the Tasaday were faring well, that their population was twenty-five, and that Lobo had grown into a strong and healthy young man.

JOHN NANCE was among the journalists included in the early expedi-
tions to gather information on the Tasaday, shortly after news of the
existence of this Stone Age group reached the outside world. He recorded
his findings in an award-winning book for adults, *The Gentle Tasaday*, and
in numerous newspaper and magazine articles.

Mr. Nance has traveled widely in Europe, the Middle East, North
Africa, India, and Australia, and spent twelve years in Asia. After several
years covering the Vietnam War and Southeast Asia, he served as bureau
chief/correspondent for the Associated Press in Manila. He now lives in
Portland, Oregon, with his wife and two children.